WORKBOOK
The Whole Body Reset

By Stephen Perrine

With Heidi Skolnik

XtraPress

Note to Reader:

Hello there!

Thanks for purchasing this companion book to **The Whole Body Reset by Stephen Perrine with Heidi Skolnik.** This book has been carefully written to take you deeper into the main text, opening new insights to help enrich your experience of the main book. It gives you the needed tools to practically apply the mind-blowing message or lessons from the main text.

Disclaimer: This book is not a replacement for medical consultations or advice from a trained professional.

How to Use This Workbook

Before proceeding with this book, it is extremely important that you should have already purchased the main book.

Please note that this book is only a supplementary guide and cannot be used independently. If you have not purchased the main book, kindly do so.

One reason for writing this book is to expand your understanding of each chapter with exercises that should deliver life-changing positive transformations in your daily life.

As you attempt each exercise or question, it is important that you avoid rushing. Rather, take your time and think critically on your answer, referring to the same section of the main book where necessary. Freely express yourself and remain truthful in your answers because no one is judging you.

When you are done with this book, keep it as a companion and try to refer back to it to see just how far you have come and the progress you have made in applying the different answers you put down.

Stay dedicated, thoughtful, enthusiastic and committed and you're sure to reap great rewards from this book.

This book would;

- ✓ Enable you change the way you think about food
- ✓ Help you make simple changes to the way you eat in order to halt or reverse weight gain and muscle loss as a result of aging.
- ✓ Understand the power of protein timing
- ✓ Enhance and highlight the main ideas and concepts from the book
- ✓ Build your mental strength
- ✓ Equip you with practical skillsets
- ✓ Make it easier for you to take action and implement lessons
- ✓ and so much more...

Table of contents

INTRODUCTION

Is a flat belly at 50 possible? Yes.

You can achieve it with the right nutrition. You need to understand the changing needs of your body as you age. Give your body just what it needs; enough proteins and fiber amongst other nutrients and exercise.

Home cooking is one way to take control over the quality and quantity of nutrition you get. Even if you're a vegetarian or vegan, you can find a way around the recipes provided to meet your nutritional needs.

The Whole Body Reset exercise routines have been designed to meet individual levels of daily activity.

The Whole Body Reset program will help you defy aging to live a healthy, happy and long life.

CHAPTER 1

THE AGE-DEFYING MAGIC OF PROTEIN TIMING

Crucial Lessons, Points and Highlights

o If you are struggling with your weight, you are not alone.
o Weight-loss diets are more potent when they are designed for your age and body type.
o As people grow older, nutrient absorption reduces.
o Consistency and nutrient consciousness is important.
o Protein timing is majorly about consuming the right amounts of essential nutrients.
o Protein timing is crucial to maintaining a lean, healthy, and disease-free life.
o The whole body reset promises weight loss without rebounds.
o Protein timing helps to prevent high blood pressure, cholesterol counts, and blood sugar.

Exercise/Questions

How is the whole body rest diet different from other diet plans?

_____

_____

_____
_____
_____
_____
_____
_____

What are the problems associated with traditional weight
loss programs?

_____
_____
_____
_____
_____
_____
_____

What is the role of muscles in preventing belly fat?

_____
_____
_____
_____
_____
_____
_____
_____

_____
_____
_____
_____
_____
_____
_____
_____
_____
_____

What is the protein requirement for men?

_____
_____
_____
_____
_____
_____
_____
_____

What is the protein requirement for women?

_____
_____
_____
_____

_____

_____

_____

_____

_____

_____

What are the plant protein sources you know?

_____

_____

_____

_____

_____

_____

_____

What are the animal protein sources you know?

_____

_____

_____

_____

_____

_____

_____

Personal Goals and Action Plans

_____
_____
_____
_____
_____
_____
_____
_____

Other Notes

_____
_____
_____
_____
_____
_____
_____
_____
_____
_____
_____
_____
_____
_____

CHAPTER 2

OUR CHANGING BODIES, OUR CHANGING NEEDS

Crucial Lessons, Points and Highlights

o   Old and young people have different responses to the food they eat.
o   Physical activity is a minority in our daily calorie burn.
o   At age forty, people begin to lose 3-8% of their muscle mass each decade.
o   A lack of muscle mass and strength increases the risks of injury and death.
o   Metabolism is not the major factor for weight gain.
o   The loss of muscle causes weight gain.
o   A lack of muscle puts people at risk of diseases, injury, and death.
o   When the muscles wither, life gets more enjoyable for the aged.

Exercise/Questions

How are muscles important?

_____
_____
_____
_____

_____
_____
_____
_____
_____
_____

What are the building blocks of muscles?

_____
_____
_____
_____
_____
_____

The process by which muscles are formed is known as?

_____
_____
_____
_____

What causes a reduction in muscular strength and function as people age?

_____
_____

_____
_____
_____
_____
_____
_____

How can muscle loss result in death?

_____
_____
_____
_____
_____
_____
_____

Why is diet restriction an important factor in the whole
body reset program?

_____
_____
_____
_____
_____
_____
_____

Personal Goals and Action Plans

_____

_____

_____

_____

_____

_____

_____

Other Notes

_____

_____

_____

_____

_____

_____

_____

_____

_____

_____

_____

_____

_____

CHAPTER 3

LET'S SPEND A DAY IN THE WHOLE BODY RESET

Crucial Lessons, Points and Highlights

o If your goal is to lose weight, then you would need to adjust your calorie intake.

o Calorie estimates are suggestions and not rules for every individual.

o Breakfast is the most important meal of the day.

o Intermittent fasting has inconclusive benefits in humans.

o For strength and vitality at old age, you must start your day with a high-protein and fiber-packed breakfast.

o The whole body reset diet makes people unconsciously reduce their sugar intake.

o For longevity, fried potatoes should be taken in limited quantities.

o People often make their diet mistakes at lunch when they are at work.

Exercise/Questions

What is the calorie requirement for men?

_____

_____

_____

_____

_____

_____

What is the total calorie requirement for women?

_____

_____

_____

_____

What is the most common diet mistake people make?

_____

_____

_____

_____

_____

_____

_____

_____

How does water intake come into play?

_____

_____

_____

_____

_____

_____

_____

_____

_____

_____

How do you avoid binge eating during the day?

_____

_____

_____

_____

_____

_____

_____

_____

When do people make their biggest nutritional mistakes?

_____

_____

_____

_____

_____

_____

_____

_____

Personal Goals and Action Plans

_____
_____
_____
_____
_____
_____
_____

Other Notes

_____
_____
_____
_____
_____
_____
_____
_____
_____
_____
_____
_____
_____

CHAPTER 4

THE SIX SIMPLE SECRETS OF BETTER HEALTH

Crucial Lessons, Points and Highlights

○ Proteins help to suppress hunger.

○ Always read labels to know the actual constituents of foods.

○ As people age, the ability to synthesize vitamin D from the sun declines.

○ Women, especially, should always ensure they have a dietary source of vitamin B folate.

○ Berries help to improve brain cognition.

○ Increasing fiber intake helps to promote weight loss.

○ Stop trying to eat less fat but eat healthier fat.

○ Instead of soda, drink water.

Exercise/Questions

What are the nine essentials amino acids required by the body?

_____

_____

_____

_____

_____

_____

_____

_____

_____

_____

_____

Why do vegans have to combine different plants?

_____

_____

_____

_____

_____

_____

_____

List the cruciferous vegetables you know.

_____

_____

_____

_____

_____

_____

_____

_____

_____

What are the three sources of healthy fat?

_____

_____

_____

_____

_____

_____

Why are fruit juices often regarded as unhealthy?

_____

_____

_____

_____

_____

How is water important in the body?

_____

_____

_____

_____

_____

_____

_____

Personal Goals and Action Plans

_____
_____
_____
_____
_____
_____
_____
_____

Other Notes

_____
_____
_____
_____
_____
_____
_____
_____
_____
_____
_____
_____
_____
_____
_____

CHAPTER 5

THE INSIDE STORY OF YOUR GUT

Crucial Lessons, Points and Highlights

o Belly fat cells can contribute to diabetes and weight gain.
o An expanding waistline in older adults is a signal of poor health.
o Inflammation contributes to reducing muscle volume and must be prevented.
o Vitamin B6 and B12 help in protein synthesis and the management of inflammation.
o People with a large amount of belly fat in their forties stand more risk of dementia in their seventies.
o Harmful lifestyle habits are destroying your essential microbiome.
o Fiber is needed for your gut microbiome to protect you.
o The whole body reset focuses on increasing the absorption of beneficial nutrients.

Exercise/Questions

How do belly fat cells contribute to weight gain?

_____
_____
_____
_____

_____

_____

_____

_____

_____

_____

What nutrients are responsible for the management of inflammation?

_____

_____

_____

_____

_____

_____

What two changes in our stomach are responsible for malabsorption and inflammation?

_____

_____

_____

_____

_____

_____

_____

Why should people be concerned about malabsorption in their fifties?

_____
_____
_____
_____
_____
_____
_____
_____
_____

What is the importance of fiber to the body?

_____
_____
_____
_____
_____
_____
_____
_____

How many fiber-rich foods are in your diet?

_____
_____
_____
_____

Personal Goals and Action Plans

_____

_____

_____

_____

_____

_____

_____

Other Notes

_____

_____

_____

_____

_____

_____

_____

_____

_____

_____

_____

_____

CHAPTER 6

HOW THE WHOLE BODY RESET CAN HELP FIGHT DISEASES AND SAVE YOUR LIFE (OVER AND AGAIN)

Crucial Lessons, Points and Highlights

o Gaining control over your food and weight gives you control over your health as well.
o If you can lower chronic inflammation, you will be less impacted by many infectious diseases.
o Stress, smoking, lack of sleep, exercise poor diet, and other bad habits contribute to chronic inflammation.
o Natural, unrefined food is the best nutrition for your body.
o Diabetes and heart diseases are inflammatory diseases.
o The whole body reset diet helps to boost immunity.
o Reduced mobility is one of the greatest vulnerabilities of aged people.
o Skipping breakfast increases the chances of diabetes.

Exercise/Questions

What are the three major benefits of the whole body reset diet?

_____

_____

_____

_____

_____

_____

_____

_____

_____

_____

What foods are you consuming that can increase inflammation?

_____

_____

_____

_____

_____

What foods are you consuming that can reduce inflammation?

_____

_____

_____

_____

_____

_____

_____

What are the advantages of natural foods?

_____
_____
_____
_____
_____
_____
_____

What are the risks of immobility and lack of exercise in aged people?

_____
_____
_____
_____
_____
_____

What dietary changes do you need to make to prevent diseases?

_____
_____
_____
_____
_____
_____

Personal Goals and Action Plans

_____
_____
_____
_____
_____
_____
_____
_____

Other Notes

_____
_____
_____
_____
_____
_____
_____
_____
_____
_____
_____
_____
_____
_____

CHAPTER 7

HOW THE WHOLE BODY RESET CAN HELP KEEP YOUR MIND SHARP

Crucial Lessons, Points and Highlights

o There is a strong relationship between nutrition and brain function.
o Check your blood pressure regularly.
o It is never too late to start improving your diet.
o For good brain health, eat regularly and do not skip breakfasts.
o It's more effective to get nutrients from food than from supplements.
o You need to be mindful of the sugar content of energy drinks, fruit juices, and other sugary drinks.
o To reduce salt intake, you need to limit the consumption of fast foods.
o With every meal, you have the power to make the healthiest diet choices.

Exercise/Questions

Why is the nutrient in food more preferable to supplements?

_____
_____

_____

_____

_____

_____

_____

_____

_____

_____

How does the whole body reset reduce sugar intake?

_____

_____

_____

_____

_____

_____

_____

What are the harmful effects of salt?

_____

_____

_____

_____

_____

_____

What's the difference between extra virgin olive oil and everyday olive oil?

_____
_____
_____
_____
_____
_____
_____

How does a low muscle mass affect the body?

_____
_____
_____
_____
_____
_____
_____

Is your current diet supportive or injurious to your brain's health?

_____
_____
_____
_____

Personal Goals and Action Plans

_____

_____

_____

_____

_____

_____

_____

_____

Other Notes

_____

_____

_____

_____

_____

_____

_____

_____

_____

_____

_____

_____

_____

_____

_____

CHAPTER 8

YOUR MAGIC SUPERMARKET LABEL DECODER

Crucial Lessons, Points and Highlights

o   Whole foods are the best diet options.
o   To avoid getting distracted from making healthy choices, always make a list before going to the grocery store.
o   The healthiest meals have higher protein and fiber than sugar.
o   You must get used to reading labels and checking out the protein, fiber, and sugar contents.
o   Products labeled as "diet" often have fewer calories and fewer nutrients.
o   Cooking meat at home is the healthier option.
o   You need to learn the meaning of the strange words found on food labels.
o   Always check out the USDA recommendations for food to guide your purchase.

Exercise/Questions

How effective is your grocery shopping list?

_____

_____

_____

_____

_____

_____

_____

_____

What are added sugars?

_____

_____

_____

_____

_____

_____

What does multigrain mean?

_____

_____

_____

_____

_____

_____

_____

Dark chocolate bars have less sugar than protein and fiber but are they good for us?

_____
_____
_____
_____
_____
_____

Why is it better to cook your meat at home?

_____
_____
_____
_____
_____
_____

How do you identify healthy extra virgin oil?

_____
_____
_____
_____
_____
_____
_____

Personal Goals and Action Plans

_____
_____
_____
_____
_____
_____
_____
_____

Other Notes

_____
_____
_____
_____
_____
_____
_____
_____
_____
_____
_____
_____
_____
_____

CHAPTER 9

TAKE YOUR WHOLE BODY OUT TO EAT

Crucial Lessons, Points and Highlights

- o Traditional diets fail because they restrict people from eating out.
- o Fast food outlets are not as unhealthy as people believe.
- o You can carry along a piece of fruit or nuts to add fiber to your diet when eating out.
- o You can design your Whole Body Reset meal using the guide before going to your favorite restaurants.

Exercise/Questions

Why are restaurant foods tagged as unhealthy?

_____

_____

_____

_____

_____

_____

_____

_____

_____
_____
_____
_____

Do your favorite meals meet your dietary requirement?

_____
_____
_____
_____
_____

How can you adjust them to meet the required standard?

_____
_____
_____
_____
_____
_____
_____
_____
_____
_____
_____

Personal Goals and Action Plans

_____
_____
_____
_____
_____
_____
_____
_____

Other Notes

_____
_____
_____
_____
_____
_____
_____
_____
_____
_____
_____
_____
_____

CHAPTER 10

TOSS OUT YOUR OLD DIET BOOKS

Crucial Lessons, Points and Highlights

o The current RDA for protein is too low for older people.
o Many people experience bloating or other side effects when they eat too much fiber, 30g a day is best.
o Most diets are created for the general public and don't take into consideration the needs of the mature physique.
o Most weight-loss programs are geared toward short-term results at the expense of long-term wellness.
o Knowing what to eat is one thing; eating what you know to be healthy is something different.
o If a diet starts becoming too weird, let common sense be your guide.
o People who fall prey to mindless snacking can try cognitive-behavioral therapies.
o You can work with a qualified professional who can help you tailor a food plan that works for you.

Exercise/Questions

Why is keto-dieting said to lead to rebound weight gain?

_____
_____

_____
_____
_____
_____
_____
_____
_____
_____
_____

Why are keto and intermittent fasting diets not recommended for people in their fifties?

_____
_____
_____
_____
_____
_____

Why is the blue zone diet not completely okay for you?

_____
_____
_____
_____
_____
_____
_____

Why is the whole30 diet unsustainable?

_____
_____
_____
_____
_____
_____
_____
_____

How many unsuccessful diets programs have you engaged in?

_____
_____
_____
_____

How do you avoid getting mixed up in a confusing diet?

_____
_____
_____
_____
_____
_____
_____

Personal Goals and Action Plans

Other Notes

CHAPTER 11

THE METABOLISM MYTH

Crucial Lessons, Points and Highlights

o   With or without exercise, the number of calories you burn per day is constant.

o   Restricting calories causes weight gain in the long run.

o   Sitting all day with no physical activity is as hazardous to your health as obesity and smoking.

o   We are all athletes and as an athlete, you need to train your body.

o   The more you simply move during the day, the healthier you'll be.

o   Exercise helps to prevent many diseases.

o   Exercise helps prevent cognitive decline and maintains brain sharpness.

o   Exercise reduces your risk of injury and has positive impacts on the microbiome.

Exercise/Questions

What is metabolism?

_____

_____

_____

_____
_____
_____
_____
_____
_____

What is the negative effect of restricting calories?

_____
_____
_____
_____
_____
_____
_____

What is exercise?

_____
_____
_____
_____
_____
_____
_____
_____
_____

What are the dangers of sitting all day with no physical activity?

_____

_____

_____

_____

_____

_____

Why should you exercise?

_____

_____

_____

_____

_____

_____

_____

What are the three types of exercises?

_____

_____

_____

_____

_____

_____

Personal Goals and Action Plans

_____

_____

_____

_____

_____

_____

_____

_____

Other Notes

_____

_____

_____

_____

_____

_____

_____

_____

_____

_____

_____

_____

_____

_____

_____

CHAPTER 12

THE WHOLE BODY FITNESS PLAN

Crucial Lessons, Points and Highlights

o When exercising, start easy to establish a routine, quality and intensity will come in thereafter.

o It is important to keep challenging yourself when exercising.

o When you push yourself enough to feel that increase in breathing, you're getting an aerobic workout.

o The Whole Body Reset strength/resistance exercises should be done 2-3 times a day so the body can recover after each season.

o Squats are crucial for independence as people age since the glutes and muscles of the upper leg makes up a large amount of muscle in our body.

o Once you get into the habit of fitness, it's a lot easier to stick with it.

o Squats and farmers' walk are the two most effective core exercises.

o Getting a partner you can be accountable to will help you achieve your exercise goals.

Exercise/Questions

What are the benefits of High intense interval training?

_____
_____
_____
_____
_____
_____
_____
_____

What are the benefits of cardio exercises?

_____
_____
_____
_____
_____
_____
_____
_____

What is core training?

_____
_____
_____
_____
_____

What are the reasons that can stop you from working out steadily?

_____
_____
_____
_____
_____
_____
_____

How can you make it easier to achieve your exercise goals?

_____
_____
_____
_____
_____
_____
_____

What are the benefits of keeping a workout diary?

_____
_____
_____
_____
_____
_____

Personal Goals and Action Plans

_____
_____
_____
_____
_____
_____
_____
_____
_____

Other Notes

_____
_____
_____
_____
_____
_____
_____
_____
_____
_____
_____
_____
_____
_____

CHAPTER 13

TROUBLESHOOTING THE WHOLE BODY RESET

Crucial Lessons, Points and Highlights

o Whole Body Reset is designed for lifelong health, mobility, and energy.

o Whey protein; a part of milk, is seen as the king of all protein.

o The Whole Body Reset is not a typical weight-loss program.

o Always recognize how hungry you are before you reach for food. Eating is best when accompanied by a feeling of hunger.

o If you're craving food, try drinking a large glass of water, and see if the craving doesn't pass in a few minutes.

o If you're eating to manage difficult emotions, consider reaching out to someone with whom you can share those feelings

o Exercise is associated with a positive outlook.

o The more time you spend on your feet, the more myokines your muscles release, and the more helpful they can be in fighting disease.

What's your opinion on rapid weight loss?

_____
_____
_____
_____
_____
_____
_____
_____
_____

How do you meet your daily goals when you have to eat out at an event?

_____
_____
_____
_____
_____
_____

What is mindless eating?

_____
_____
_____
_____
_____

How do you stop eating mindless eating?

_____

_____

_____

_____

_____

_____

_____

_____

Can vegans use the Whole Body Reset?

_____

_____

_____

_____

How can you incorporate exercise into your intense workdays?

_____

_____

_____

_____

_____

_____

_____

_____

Personal Goals and Action Plans

Other Notes

CHAPTER 14

WHOLE BODY RECIPES

Crucial Lessons, Points and Highlights

o Cooking at home helps to stop age-related waistline increment.
o Loading your diet with nutritionally dense food is more important than cutting calories.
o If you don't eat enough protein in the morning, you're probably going to be in muscle breakdown all day long.
o If cooking seems time-consuming or overwhelming, make as much as you can ahead of time.
o Ginger is well known for its ability to soothe an upset stomach and nausea but is also good for oral health.
o Cinnamon reduces inflammation
o Snacking should be based on needs, hunger, and activity.

Exercise/Questions

How can you ensure you cook your meals if you have a busy schedule?

_____
_____

_____

_____

_____

_____

_____

_____

What's the disadvantage of eating at restaurants?

_____

_____

_____

_____

_____

_____

_____

Why is breakfast the most important meal of the day?

_____

_____

_____

_____

_____

_____

_____

_____

Why are nutritionally dense foods important?

_____

_____

_____

_____

_____

_____

_____

_____

How can you make your oatmeal more enjoyable?

_____

_____

_____

_____

_____

_____

Why is it better to make your sauces and salads?

_____

_____

_____

_____

_____

_____

Personal Goals and Action Plans

_____
_____
_____
_____
_____
_____
_____
_____

Other Notes

_____
_____
_____
_____
_____
_____
_____
_____
_____
_____
_____
_____
_____
_____
_____

Made in the USA
Middletown, DE
07 April 2022